SONGS FROM A SINGLE EYE

NEW DIRECTIONS POETRY PAMPHLETS

SONGS FROM
A SINGLE EYE

Oswald von Wolkenstein

TRANSLATED FROM THE MIDDLE HIGH GERMAN
WITH VITA AND NOTES BY RICHARD SIEBURTH

FOREWORD BY SIEGFRIED WALTER DE RACHEWILTZ

NEW DIRECTIONS POETRY PAMPHLET #27

Cover design by Erik Carter
Text design by Erik Rieselbach
Manufactured in the United States of America
New Directions Books are printed on acid-free paper
First published as New Directions Poetry Pamphlet #27 in 2019

Library of Congress Cataloging-in-Publication Data
Names: Wolkenstein, Oswald von, 1377?–1445, author. | Sieburth, Richard, translator. | Rachewiltz, Siegfried de, 1947– writer of foreword.
Title: Songs from a single eye / Oswald von Wolkenstein ; translated from the Middle High German with vita and notes by Richard Sieburth ; foreword by Siegfried Walter de Rachewiltz.
Description: New York, NY : New Directions Publishing Corporation, 2019. | Series: New Directions poetry pamphlet ; #27 | Translated from the Middle High German.
Identifiers: LCCN 2019026075 | ISBN 9780811229012 (paperback ; acid-free paper)
Classification: LCC PT1695.W4 A275 2019 | DDC 831/.3—dc23
LC record available at https://lccn.loc.gov/2019026075

10 9 8 7 6 5 4 3 2 1

New Directions Books are published for James Laughlin
by New Directions Publishing Corporation
80 Eighth Avenue, New York 10011

ndbooks.com

Foreword: What's in a Name?

The story has been told before, but from a slightly different angle.

As far as I am concerned, it began in the summer of 1946, when I was first conceived (of). At that time my mother was entertaining the thought of making a living for herself and her future family by learning how to carve intaglios from Herr Bacher and—partly inspired by Ronald Duncan's *Journal of a Husbandman*—by running a small but self-sufficient household based on the lactation and fertility of a single cow.

The cottage in Gais, which was going to house this enterprise, stood at the foot of a somber and rather uninspiring castle (as castles go in the South Tyrol), Schloss Neuhaus, first mentioned in 1248 as *castrum novum*. After the war, nobody seemed to quite know who the owner of this semi-abandoned manor was. The last owner had been Count Cäsar Strassoldo-Grafenberg, who had bought it from Johann Graf Thun in 1924. The Strassoldos were ancient nobility from Goriza / Görz and their lineage could boast of captains, crusaders, diplomats, bishops, and even some learned literati. They were loyal supporters of the Habsburgs and supplied them with sundry generals and even a governor: Michael Strassoldo was governor of Lombardy and brother-in-law of Field Marshal Radetzky. In 1939 they must have opted for Germany, which would explain why Schloss Neuhaus was "acquired" by the Ente Nazionale per le Tre Venezie in 1942. Founded originally in 1919 as the Istituto per la Rinascita Agraria, this governmental agency during the *era fascista* was in charge of managing property that had been expropriated from foreign nationals or acquired from those Tyroleans who had opted for the Reich in 1939. (In 1957 Count Strassoldo was allowed to "buy back" Neuhaus, which he promptly resold to a Swiss dentist.)

Having received some vague permission to inhabit the shady stronghold, my parents moved into Neuhaus just in time for a solitary celebration of the first postwar Christmas of 1946.

As with all castles, there were legends and vague reminiscences that came with the place. These my mother diligently reported back to Ezra Pound at St. Elizabeths, a "captive audience" if ever there was one.

This is how a chimerical Margarete von Taufers found her way into the *Cantos*. But Neuhaus's claim to fame was that at some point a celebrated Minnesänger had supposedly sojourned there. In those days, this could have only meant Walther von der Vogelweide, a name that everybody in the South Tyrol knew—not for having read him but because, after an over-enthusiastic scholar had set forth the totally fictitious theory that Walther was a native Tyrolean, local patriots had turned him into a symbol of the South Tyrol's age-old Germanic heritage and in 1889 had raised a monument to him in Bozen's main square, henceforth named Waltherplatz. In 1896 the Italian patriots countered with a statue of Dante in Trent. One of the measures taken by the fascist regime in its attempt to turn Bolzano into a bulwark of *italianitá* was to remove Walther's statue to a neighboring park in 1935 and to change the square's name to Piazza della Vittoria. Of course, when Italy switched sides and the German troops took over the north in 1943, the square was once again renamed after the German minstrel: "Das heisst Waltherplatz," as E. P. was told (see Canto 83) when making his way through the desolate city with his daughter in September of that year.

Then came Pisa, the bug house, and all the rest: the news that his daughter was going to live in Walther von der Vogelweide's castle (whose coat of arms was a bird in a cage) elicited an enthusiastic response from the caged panther:

> "Dearest Child—Fact of its being Walther's castello excited me almost to air mail!"

And he added instructions on how to turn the castle into a cultural haven for poets and musicians: he would dispatch Gerhard Münch and Basil Bunting to the precincts, with the latter assigned to the tending of the gardens.

Walther von der Vogelweide: for E. P. that meant Longfellow (a distant relative), whose poem about Walther and the birds singing over his tomb his mother Isabel had probably read to him as a child. It also meant Synge, whose prose translation of a song of Walther's he may have known via Yeats. But most of all it meant Ford Madox Ford, whose rendition of "Unter den Linden" he had praised back in 1913 when reviewing his *Collected Poems*: "Mr. Hueffer has also the gift for making lyrics that sing, as for example the 'Tandaradei' more or less after von der Vogelweide." (At some point

Ford claimed to have knocked off the translation when he was only twelve years old.)

> "Ciao Cara," E. P. wrote his daughter, "Dear old Fordie wd. / have been excited about it being Walther's old castello=too bad he died before he had a chance to invent 1066 misstatements on the subject."

In this case, one misstatement more or less would not have made much of a difference.

When it came to German poetry, E. P. didn't feel that there was much that was essential to his canon of Kulchur: of the Middle Ages, he retained only "Morungen, Wolfram and von der Vogelweide" as part of his Teutonic paideuma. He acknowledged Goethe's "fine" and "unapproachable" lyrics ("as good as Heine's and von der Vogelweide's") but the latter two were the only ones that seem to have elicited any real enthusiasm or translation on his part. As it turned out, Walther (in Ford's version of "Unter den Linden") was the only German poet to make it into Pound's *Confucius to Cummings* anthology (along with Martin Luther!).

When his daughter complained about how cold it was in Walther's castello, he consoled her with the poet's own verses:

> "Uns had diu Winter geskaded über al / Heide and Walde syn alle nu kal." (Quoting from memory, *val* became *kal*, though both make sense.)

Finally, when the news was broken that he would soon be a "grandpa" and he was asked to suggest a name for his grandchild, the answer was unequivocal: "There is obviously only one name, d[as].h[eisst]. Walther, in them surroundings!"

And upon learning of my arrival:

> "Evviva Walther!
> Canzone degli Uccelli. Da tagte es.
> And it has put out of head most of whatever else was to say."

The "canzone" in question referred not only to Janequin's "Le Chant des oiseaux" (whose score is reproduced in Canto 75), but probably also to the legend set to verse by Longfellow, according to which Walther's fame was kept alive by the birds about his tombstone that—in his last will and testament—he stipulated should be fed even after his death.

My father was meanwhile spinning his own ancestral fantasies, eventually deciding to name his firstborn after the Longobard king Sigifredus, and granting Walther only second place in the long slur of names that would encumber my passport and other personal documents for years to come.

No need here to go into the feud that ensued between my grandmother and my parents over this decision: it lasted over half a century, with both E. P. and Olga always insisting on calling me Walt(er) and nothing else.

BUT, if anything, the name should have been Oswald, for the one and only Minnesänger ever to reside in our home at Schloss Neuhaus was Oswald von Wolkenstein, who assumed the lordship of the castle around 1420.

How is it that E. P. remained in the dark about Oswald?

The medieval world, as rediscovered and largely recreated by German romanticism, could accommodate Arthurian legends and marvels, the bloody battles between cross and crescent of the Carolingian cycle, and the sound and fury of the Nibelungen. As for the first-person lyric, Walther von der Vogelweide composed masterful poems on different varieties of *Minne* as well as scathing songs against stingy patrons and papal claims to worldly power. While denouncing the demise of Christian values and ideals, he left us the most charming pastourelle ever written, "Unter den Linden." But what came after Walther was, to a large extent, epigonal and cliché-ridden imitation.

Oswald, a *quattrocento* contemporary of François Villon, appeared on the scene at the waning of the Middle Ages. He felt cheated out of his inheritance on various accounts: first, because the age into which he was born did not put great stock in his rights and privileges as a nobleman—ladies were more attracted to burghers with fat purses than to blue blood—and second, because he had been literally shortchanged by his father who in his will had left him a third of a rundown castle (Hauenstein) on a remote rock, with all the legal and illegal entanglements that came with it.

Oswald therefore set out to make his fortune elsewhere—as a knight, envoy, diplomat, and drinking companion of powerful protectors, like King (and later Holy Roman Emperor) Sigismund, whom he served during the Council of Constance that ended the Papal Schism and whom he accompanied on his "crusades" against the Hussites in the Kingdom of Bohemia. The fact that Oswald was a gifted singer and songwriter certainly contributed to his popularity in the noble and perhaps sometimes not so noble circles that he frequented—but he never sang or composed for a living. Not having to curry the favor of patrons, he remained remarkably free to perform for family and friends whatever he so damn pleased. It was out of his own pocket that, toward the end of his life, he commissioned scribes from the Augustinian priory of Neustift near Brixen to copy down both his poems and their accompanying music in an expensive parchment codex which was not rediscovered until 1800 in Vienna by a friend of Klopstock's and translator of Ossian.

But it was only in recent years—with the systematic study of his life and work having begun in the 1970s—that Oswald's genius as a poet and a composer began to be fully recognized. The main reasons that he therefore lay outside of E. P.'s ken was that international scholarship had by and large ignored him, that none of the anthologies of medieval German poetry available to Pound included any of his poems and, most of all, that no congenial translations of his work were available.

Sero therefore—too too late—came the well-intentioned gift by Wieland Schmied who in 1960, prompted by H. C. Artmann, published a selection of sixteen of Oswald's poems translated into modern German and dedicated to "il miglior fabbro" under the title *Der mit dem einem Auge*.

How ironic that the late medieval poet who had breathed life into poetic genres that in his time had become stale cream-puffs and who had regenerated German by infusing it with a new, experimental vocabulary drawn from his Tyrolean vernacular and from the many lingos and languages he had picked up in his travels; how ironic that the one composer who had revolutionized German songwriting by introducing polyphony and fusing the various musical styles he had encountered in his journeys abroad; in short, how ironic that the first truly "modern" poet in German literature should have escaped E. P.'s attention.

The castle that Pound's daughter had inhabited and where his mother

Isabel eventually died was not "Walther's castello" but in fact one of the residences of a poet who like few before him had turned his life into art, his biography into song—whether it be in the persona of the belligerent swashbuckler, the lusty lover, the doting husband, the merry carouser, the rueful sinner, the prudent politician, or the world-weary old man.

The following selection of Oswald in English has been undertaken by my old friend Richard Sieburth in homage to E. P.'s (and Paul Blackburn's) versions of the troubadours—and, more specifically to mark the auspicious ninetieth birthday of Pound's daughter Mary, for whom this volume was initially published in a limited edition by Medus in Meran/o in 2015. The melopoeia of these translations speaks to our contemporary ear, giving us an Oswald somewhere between the cadences of a Bob Dylan and the raw urgencies of rap.

—SIEGFRIED WALTER DE RACHEWILTZ

A note on this edition

The poems gathered here, identified by their classic 1962 Klein edition (or "K.") numbers, represent but a small fraction of the three hundred-plus songs that have come down to us. Oswald wrote in many modes and genres: dawn-songs or albas, May songs, lover's laments, songs of praise and gratitude, dance songs, hunting and fowling songs, pastourelles, eclogues, propaganda songs (against the Hussites), devotional songs dedicated to the Virgin Mary, etc. The ten poems that I have chosen to translate—for the most part the first-person narrative poems dating from O.'s forties (1417–27)—stand out from the rest of his corpus because they allow us to witness the emergence of the first distinctively "modern" autobiographical voice in German verse. The "Ich Wolkenstein" ("I, Wolkenstein") who appears in these songs is not just a conventional poetic persona, but also the legal signatory of any number of court documents and the illustrious name of a historical subject who was (according to numerous archives) a significant actor on the contemporary political stage. The pronoun "I" (or grammatical variants of it) occurs over two thousand times in O.'s corpus, but it is a new kind of "I"—an "I" who wants (like any modern folk singer or rapper) to be heard by his audience as credibly *referring* to the *real* events of a lived life, an "I" whose adventurous exploits can be corroborated by the citation of *actual* persons and places known to his listeners. O. is therefore often compared to his contemporary François Villon—especially in the various caustic (and proto-Brechtian) poems he composed while in jail. Unlike Villon, however, O. was still very much a part of the troubadour (or *Minnesänger*) tradition. That is: he *sang* his poems aloud (probably a cappella, or perhaps strumming a lute) to tunes that he had either borrowed or newly devised.

For musicologists, O. is above all remembered as one of the very first German composers to have introduced (French and Italian) polyphony into his songs. Although none of these polyphonic songs have been translated here, O.'s poetry, even when monophonic, is always multivoiced, always stereo. German is what linguists call a "pluricentric" language: the Middle High German in which O. performs his dialectal "stylings" (as one might say of a jazz vocalist) is a Bavarian-Southern Austrian variant of the broader German "roof language" (*Decksprache*) of the period, to which he however adds further lexical grace notes of Rhinelandish and Allemannic. O. boasted of having learned ten tongues over the course of his travels: his heteroglossia is most obvious in the two macaronic (and very Joycean) poems included at the end of this volume. Where O. proves the most plurivocal, however, is in his deployment of (self-)irony, particularly when it comes to his sarcastic (and counter-Petrarchan) deployment of the clichés of courtly love. Pound would have been delighted to have discovered in O. the most Laforguian of the late troubadours. He would have also immediately seized on O.'s practice of *motz el son*—the performative amalgam of word and tune.

I have followed the 2007 Reclam edition of O.'s *Lieder* by printing examples of Brunner's modernized scorings of his music (transposed into the key of G) as the "originals" to which my English translations were attuned. I first learned to listen to O.'s cadences over the course of any number of long (and wine-soaked) evenings with my old friend Sizzo de Rachewiltz— who for more than forty years has acted as a precious native informant on all things Tyrolean (and Poundian). I also lent a rapt ear to counter-tenor Andreas Scholl's interpretations of these songs—whose melismata are amazing—and subsequently delved into Dieter Kühn's 1977 biography of the poet, *Ich Wolkenstein*, on which the Vita is based. In preparing these translations, I further consulted the modern German versions of O.'s poems by Wachinger, Spechtler, Kühn, and Ruiss. A complete translation of O. into English was published by Albrecht Classen in 2008 (Palgrave / Macmillan). It provides a valuable, scholarly trot to the poems, but is not really the place to go listen to O.'s particular music. My thanks to David Georgi and Peter Cole for rereading earlier versions of these translations, and helping to raise them to the level of song. My greatest debt, however, goes out to the ear of Basil Bunting, in his great prison poem, "Villon."

—R. S.

Vita

1377 Oswald von Wolkenstein born to Friedrich von Wolkenstein and Katharina von Villanders in Schöneck (or perhaps Trostburg) Castle, about fifty kilometers northeast of Bozen in the county of Tyrol.

1387 Age ten, O. leaves home, presumably to become a squire to a knight errant. His later poems mention youthful travels to Prussia, Lithuania, the eastern Mediterranean, Turkey, Crimea, and the Black Sea.

1400 At the death of his father, O. returns to the Tyrol to claim his inheritance, but his older brother Michael declines to execute the will until their younger brother Leonhard has reached maturity.

1401 O. enters into the service of Rupert, the Rhinegrave of the Palatinate, elected King of Germany the previous year, and joins him on an ill-fated campaign in Italy where he hopes to be officially crowned Holy Roman Emperor by Pope Boniface IX. After his defeat at Brescia, Rupert retreats to Germany, where he dies in 1410. He is succeeded by Sigismund of Luxemburg in 1411—who will eventually become O.'s second major royal patron.

1404 Anxious to get his hands on property he deems rightfully his, O. robs a chest of precious stones from his older brother. When the latter discovers the theft, O. accuses Michael's wife of having stolen the jewels with the help of her lover. In addition, he also apparently attempts to embezzle ground rents owed to his older brother. According to contemporary accounts, Michael then tries to run O. through with a sword and forces him to publicly confess to his misdeeds.

1406 Frederick IV, the young Habsburg Duke of Austria, takes over as the newly named Count of Tyrol, encountering fierce opposition from the local landed gentry of the region—particularly from the fractious and independent-minded Wolkenstein family.

1407 Now thirty, O. finally receives his share of the family inheritance: one-third of the rundown castle of Hauenstein and its associated estates in Seis am Schlern. The other two-thirds of the castle belong to the knight Martin Jäger, who resides three days away in Meran. Exercising his *Faustrecht* ("law of the fist") in typical robber-baron fashion, O. takes advantage of the latter's absentee ownership to occupy the entire castle and to appropriate the tithes of all its tenant farmers. In an extravagant display of both his piety and power as a new local lord of the region, O. dedicates a chapel at nearby Brixen to his patron saint, Oswald—whom he claims had saved him from shipwreck in the Black Sea by miraculously providing him with a cask of Malvasia wine on which he safely floated to shore. He memorializes this incident, mentioned several times in his poetry, in a mural designed for the chapel—now long lost. He also adorns the chapel with a near-life-sized bas-relief of himself in the garb of a crusader and wearing a long beard, the traditional insignia of a male pilgrim. Rediscovered in 1847, this statue is now mounted on a wall of the cloister of Brixen. Around this same time O. begins writing love songs for Anna Hausmann, the wife of a prosperous Brixner burgher and the Lady in whose chivalric service he claims to have undertaken his pilgrimage to the Holy Land in 1409–10, where, according to a number of his poems, he visited both Bethlehem and the Holy Sepulchre.

1414 In the wake of the Western Schism of 1378, there are now three claimants to the papacy: Gregory XII (Rome), antipope Benedict XIII (Avignon), and antipope John XXIII (Pisa). In his official capacity as the King of the Romans and imperial protector of the church, Sigismund convenes the Council of Constance in late 1414. Its goals: to put an end to the schism by installing a new compromise pope in Rome (Martin V); to rid the church of the heretical followers of John Wycliffe and Jan Hus (who, having been lured there and granted immunity, is treacherously burned at the stake at Constance the following year); and to resolve the years of frontier warfare between the Teutonic Knights and the "heathen" Polish-Lithuanians.

1415 O. arrives in Constance in early February, initially as the privy counselor to the bishop of Brixen and then employed as an advisor to King Sigismund. A month later, Sigismund dispatches O. on a diplomatic mission whose itinerary is variously described in his poetry: he may have traveled to Lisbon via England, Scotland, and Ireland, or he may have proceeded directly to Portugal, where he joins King John's victorious expedition in August against the Moorish stronghold of Ceuta on the coast of northern Africa before returning to Perpignan to meet up with King Sigismund, the Queen of Aragon, and antipope Benedict.

1416 End of schism celebrated with Sigismund in Avignon in early January. O. accompanies his king to Paris in March, where he registers the events of his visit to the French court and to the Sorbonne in a clownish, semi-obscene poem worthy of Villon. Sigismund continues on to England in order to negotiate a diplomatic end to the Hundred Years' War in the wake of Agincourt, but urgently dispatches O. back to Constance, where Duke Frederick of Austria has just escaped from the house arrest imposed on him by Sigismund for having helped antipope John flee the city the previous year. O. lives in Constance for over a year, composing over forty songs for the amusement of a receptive German-speaking (and multilingual) audience—these songs comprise nearly a third of his total poetic output.

1417 Sigismund rejoins O. in Constance, and places Frederick of Austria under imperial ban, stripping him of his territories in Baden and Switzerland. O. marries the Bavarian noblewoman Margarete von Schwangau, who brings him a generous dowry and a title as imperial knight. She will subsequently bear him seven children and appears affectionately in his erotic songs as Gret, Gretlein, or Gredli (to his Oesli).

1418 O. returns to the Tyrol to take up residence in Hauenstein with his new wife. Joins the league of local nobles known as the Elefantenbund ("elephant federation") who are violently opposed to Duke Frederick of Austria and who instead pledge their allegiance to the German king Sigismund, whom they consider the guarantor of their ancestral feudal rights.

1419–20 O. twice travels to Hungary to join Sigismund, now king of both Bohemia and Hungary, in his (disastrous) campaigns against the Hussites.

1421 In September, O. is lured by his (ex-?) lover Anna Hausmann to a rendezvous where he is ambushed, bound, and imprisoned by his Hauenstein enemy Martin Jäger in the Fahlburg and Forst castles near Meran. Three months later Jäger hands O. over to his archnemesis Frederick, who keeps him in captivity in Innsbruck until March of the following year. During these seven months of imprisonment, O. writes some of his most powerful and plangent poems.

1422 In March, Frederick, in exchange for the exorbitant bail of 6,000 ducats (provided by the Wolkenstein family and its in-laws) liberates O., giving him five months to settle his financial affairs with Jäger. O. fails to show up for his court hearing at Schloss Tirol in August and instead rides to Hungary/Bohemia to join Sigismund at his court at Pressburg (Bratislava).

1423 Together with his two brothers, and backed by Sigismund, O. falls back on the castle of Greifenstein to a launch a full-scale rebellion against Frederick. After a lengthy siege, the latter, aided by the local peasantry and burghers, manages to break the resistance of the band of refractory nobles holed up in the castle—a Tyrolean Alamo memorialized in one of O.'s most famous poems.

1425 Sigismund, finding himself overextended in three wars, finally makes peace with his Austrian rival Frederick. Now living at Castle Neuhaus near Gais, which lay within the dominions of the counts of Görz (and thus out of the reach of his Habsburg foe), O. commissions the scribes at the nearby Neustift Monastery to create a manuscript of all his songs to date. Known as Ms. A, it contains 108 poems, arranged in chronological and/or thematic order. Thirty-nine of its songs are polyphonic, sixteen of which are based on *ars nova* compositions inspired by Guillaume de Machaut that O. may have first heard during his travels in France or Italy. Death of his Lady, Anna Hausmann.

1426–27 Still feuding with Frederick, O. attempts to flee the Tyrol but is arrested and imprisoned by the latter in Castle Vellenberg in Innsbruck. As a condition for his release after several months in jail, O. is forced to pay Jäger back for all his stolen tithes and to swear fealty to Frederick, in return for which he finally receives the remaining two-thirds of Hauenstein.

1428 Journeys to Cologne, where he becomes involved in further political intrigues against the bishop of Brixen and becomes a member of the Geheimgericht ("secret court").

1431 With his brother Michael, O. attends the Diet of Nuremberg (or Reichstag), where he is awarded the highest rank of the Order of the Dragon in recognition of his imperial service to Sigismund. Participates in the ongoing wars against the Hussites in Bohemia. Sigismund's imperial forces flee before the vastly outnumbered enemy host at Taus in August. Joan of Arc burned at the stake. François Villon born.

1432 O. again has his poems and music transcribed (at great expense) by the scribes of Neustift, this time on high-quality parchment (Ms. B)—188 poems in all, sixteen of which do not figure in Ms. A. In this manuscript, the songs are not arranged thematically or chronologically, but according to their melodies (rendered in the new French notation). This luxury edition is illustrated by a colored portrait of O. apparently executed by Pisanello or by a member of his workshop [see p. 18 of this volume]. It shows O. gloriously bedecked with the insignias of the various noble orders to which he has been named and displays his right eye as completely closed—the result (as recent autopsies of O.'s skull have concluded) of a congenitally defective socket.

1433 Sigismund finally crowned Holy Roman Emperor in Rome, with O. probably in attendance.

1437 Sigismund dies, and with him the line of the House of Luxemburg becomes extinct, thus assuring the future hegemony of the Habsburgs over Austria-Hungary and the Tyrol.

1439 Duke Frederick dies at Innsbruck. During the transitional period after his decease, O. assumes an important role as one of the five military commanders of the Tyrol and an influential member of its legislature.

1445 Having outlived all his friends and foes, O. dies during a summer heat wave in Meran at the age of sixty-eight.

WAR MUSIC

1.

Let's roll! said Michael   von Wolkenstein
After them! said Oswald   von Wolkenstein
Mount up! said Leonhard   von Wolkenstein
Drive them out   from Greifenstein

2.

All hell broke loose   scorching flames
Gore splattered   on the rocks below
Iron helmets   armor and bows
Ditched as they fled   whoops of rage

3.

Their huts and tents   and engines of war
Reduced to ashes   on the upper sward
Bad debts (they say)   come home to roost
So here, Duke Friedrich   take your reward

4.

No one could sort   the smoke of battle
From the fog of war   at Ravenstein-on-Ried
Crossbows twanging   whoosh of arrows
Nails yanked   from the ooze of marrow

5.

Peasants of St. George   the whole damn parish
Conspired against us   the whole damn bunch
Then our Ravenstein   buddies turned up
Greetings, neighbors   yes, we're in a crunch

6.

Shoving and shooting   hue and cry
Breaking out below   hear the battle whoop
My fellow knights   here we either win or lose
Mice roasting in every roof   the smell of soot

7.

The troops from Bozen   from Ritten and Meran
From Hafling and Mölten   want to cook our goose
Stouthearted men   from the Sarntal and Jenes
Let them try to entrap us   and we'll vamoose

KNIGHT ERRANT

1.

It occurred to me, when I was ten years old,
to see what the world out there might hold.
Down and out, in quarters hot and cold,
I lived amid Christians, Greeks, and heathens.

Three cents in my bag and small crusts of bread
were all I'd packed, as I forged ahead.
Among kin and foe red drops of blood I shed
and often thought I'd perish from my lesions.
I traveled on foot until my father died,
near fourteen years old, no horse in sight,
except that mare I stole, pale dun of hide,
filched from me, after one short season.
Yes, I was a courier, a cook, a stable boy,
and in Crete and elsewhere was employed,
pulling oars (by which I was near destroyed).
A smock was all I wore, whatever the region.

2.
To Prussia, Lithuania, Turkey, Tartary,
and on to France, Spain, and Lombardy,
the Love I served was always paid by me,
not by Ruprecht, Sigmund, and their eagle flags.
French, Moorish, Catalan, and Castilian,
German, Latin, Wendish, Lombard, Romansch, and Russian
were the ten tongues I mastered for discussion
and I could also fiddle, drum, trumpet, and blow the bag.
I've sailed many an isle and bay and many a land
on great ships that never foundered on the strand.
From coast to coast, from north to south I ran,
but the Black Sea, luckily, provided me a cask to grab.
That was when my brigantine was smashed to bits
and I, a merchant, floated back to shore on it,
along with some Russian, all my profits aswim
in the sea, with me hauled up safely on a crag.

3.
The Queen of Aragon was so tender and sweet.
I knelt before her, my beard most replete,
into which her white hands slipped the treat
of a ring, saying *non maiplus disligaides*.
Then in my earlobes she pierced little holes
with a needle, my virtue to extol,
into which a pair of earrings she cajoled,
It's what they here call a bangle or *raicades*.
I then sought out Sigmund, my rightful boss,
Who pulled a face and made a cross,
Saying, "Why you wearing all this foreign tosh?"
"Won't your ears be inflamed by otitis?"
Everyone there together laughed,
nine characters of the royal cast
at Perpignan, Pedro Luna with his papal staff,
plus the tenth Roman king and lady of Prades.

4.
I wanted to change my foolish life, it's true,
and traveled as a migrant monk two years through.
Devotion, at the outset, was all I knew
before my service of Love grew too dire.
Riding my steed, engaged in knightly games
I'd served a Lady (whom I'd rather not name).
She never granted me the slightest grace
until I finally agreed to play the pilgrim friar.
Things were working out, all in all,
garbed as I was in hood and cowl.
Never before or since was I so enthralled.

I thought she fully grasped my words on fire.
But all my devotion just went up in smoke
when in a fog I ditched my palmer's clothes.
Since then, love is a thing I completely loathe.
She had chilled the thrill of my desire.

5.
It would take too long to tell of all my woes.
This red mouth still holds me in its throes,
I'm still scarred, from head to toes.
In her presence, I'd drip with sweat,
my face now blushing, now almost white
as I managed to catch her roving eye.
All my tremblings and weighty sighs
have made of me a burnt-out wreck.
I often fled away from her in fright,
two hundred miles, no hope in sight,
frost, rain, and snow lacking the ice
to chill her sunburn upon my neck.
Near her, I was without midst or measure:
because of my Lady, I needed to venture
on paths of woe, sans friend or leisure,
hoping her grace might hold my hate in check.

6.
Four hundred maidens and nary a man,
whose loveliness I glimpsed on Ios land.
No finer picture at my mind's command,
though none could vie with my Lady,
whose image still weighed on my back.
If only she knew of half my wrack,

I might have gotten myself back on track
to amend the scenes of this tragedy—
wringing my hands, far from her side,
deprived of the bounty of her smile,
never sleeping, night after night,
her white arms, roots of my malady.
Love's hard to serve, O boys and girls,
don't just go out and give it a whirl.
For me, it's been the end of a world.
See what my tearful eyes have made of me.

7.
I'm forty years old, give or take two.
Having sowed my oats and sundry tunes,
it's about time I assumed fatherhood
to breed a brood of screaming kids in cribs,
even though I swear I'll never forget
the one on whom my heart was always set
and to whose joys I'll ever be in faithful debt,
while my wife goes into her usual snits.
Many a wise man has taken my advice,
many an ear has found pleasure in my lyre.
I, Wolkenstein, have definitely paid the price
for wedding my songs to this earth and admit
I've no idea what my death will be worth.
My only reward will lie in my works.
If I have served God as he truly deserves,
I'll never go in fear of the fiery pit.

PENANCE

1.

To begin it all
without fear of God,
to do it all
without conscience,
swollen with sin.

No poet in his wile
or wisdom
could carry this off
without God's assistance.
So here I am,
sick to my soul,
terrified of death,
begging you,
Holy Virgin Catherine,
to ask Mary's child
to intervene
on my behalf
and take me into his care.
I thank the Lord
(praised be He)
for granting me an ear
and allowing me
to do penance
for all my sins,
and for teaching us all
that no love is ever long
without suffering.

2.
What a picture of woman was she
to whom I devoted many a day,
thirteen years or more, I'd say,
pledged to the faithful service
of all her heart desired.
No soul on earth
did I more love or admire.

Through mountain, wood, and field
and in many a land I've ridden,
never forgetful of her charms,
my body utterly smitten,
her red mouth tearing at my heart.
Many a night and morrow
she reached out to me
with her naked arms.
She still lives in my marrow,
arm and leg and thigh,
ever mine, in sorrow.

3.
We were so in love
we barely gave a thought
to the pain it begot,
yet somehow
we could never burst
its chains.
The proof?
Here I lie
in shackles,
my life's woes
in the balance.
Because of Love,
God weighs me
by my skin and hair,
my slightest misdeed
tipping the scales.
Love makes my penance
so much worse.

I can no longer cast it
into decent verse.
Robbed of felicity,
I still lie in Love's
ropes and chains.
O Lord, no longer delay
your judgment.
The time has come
to purge my sins away.

4.
No man in his right mind
would insist, unless mad,
on resisting the path
to which he was ordained,
given that Time commands
both fortune and misfortune,
and what Time proclaims
can never be escaped.
A sinner's path is paved
with many twists and turns,
too easily earned.
No poet can put this into words.
Only God, who assigns
each man his lot,
can weigh this tiny jot
in His holy hand.
His jealous eye observes
every man and lady fair
and every creature of the earth
as they stand or fall

upon their hour.
Love and respect
are what He demands,
tributes to His higher power.
He who ignores this
falls further into sin.
God lets him run
all over the map,
then gathers him
into His trap.

5.
Love is a word
beyond leisure.
Who achieves it
beyond measure
is aware that
Love conquers all,
convincing God
to withhold the gall
from the sinner
and to promise
the solace of pleasure.
Love, sweet treasure,
how lovelessly
hast thou blinded me
to forget to honor
Him with my love,
who went through death
for me and all the other
stone-cold sinners,

leaving me to roast
in this fire of discontent.
Had I only expended
half the love on God
I so tenderly spent
on this Lady,
(so cruel, so shady),
I'd be on my way
to Judgment Day,
free of sin.
O earthly delights,
how you do us in!

6.
Only now do I bemoan
the arrogance
that incited his wrath,
he who displayed me
a measure of clemency,
unwilling though
I was to withdraw
the evil horns
that had driven me
to such trespass.
Five iron fetters
were my reward.
As was his wish,
two of them
clapped onto my feet,
one on my left arm,
a screw vised

onto my thumb,
a steel ring
strangling my neck—
which made for five,
when all was said
and done.
Then my Lady
came to visit,
proposing to nurse me
in my calamity.
O Lord,
those cold white arms,
how loveless their amity!
Though I told her
my heart was the place
that grieved me most,
she offered no remedy.
Such was the mercy
she showed me!

7.
Battered by sorrows,
my heart beats
ever more weakly
in my chest
at the bitter
thought of death,
every day, night, and morrow.
The pain takes away my breath.
Who knows where
my poor soul

will soon be housed?
O child of Mary, stand by me,
poor Wolkenstein,
in my hour of need,
shelter me in your grace.
As for those
out for my hide,
help them atone
for all the filthy crimes
they have connived
to commit against me.
Even this Lady
who has done
so much to do me in
(I swear and cross my heart)
has never inspired
a whit of hate
on my sorry part.
If from this world
I need soon depart,
I beg the Lord
(if it's not too late)
not to be too hard
on her on my account.
To what, in the end,
do we all amount?

MERCIFUL END

1.
I see and hear
so many complain
their estates
are going to rack and ruin.
Me, my only gripe's
the gone days
of my youth,
nary a care
as to where the hell

in the world
I stood.
Head-, back-, hand-, foot-
aches now
bespeak my age.
Sir Flesh, Sir Bones,
now is the season
you pay for the sins
I once committed
for no good reason.
The price?
Bloodshot eyes, ashen skin, gray hair.
Now I look before I leap,
ever more spooked by fear.
Heavy my heart, my conscience, tongue, and tread,
my every step stooped,
my every limb wed
to palsy,
and "woe is me"
now the sole song
that matters
to my days and nights,
my tenor voice
torn to tatters.

2.
Curly blond locks
once grew thick
upon my head,
now black
with silver threads
and pooled

with bald spots.
My mouth's turning blue,
unpleasing
to my love so true.
My teeth are weak and stained,
which makes it tough to chew.
All the gold in the world
couldn't make them new
or buy myself relief
longer than a dream's
brief interlude
of deceit.
Where once I ran
and leapt, I limp,
and as for singing,
short of breath,
I cough my way
through songs,
weak and useless
as I've become.
So toss me
into the cold ground
and give me rest,
that I be done
with death.

3.
From all this,
learn, young man,
not to place
your faith in beauty
or in power.

Aim your songs
of praise far higher.
I was once
what you are now.
Should you ever become
what I am today,
your good works
shall serve you well.
When all is said
and done, I need
to lead my life
at God's pleasure,
fasting, praying,
attending church,
falling on my knees,
my earthly existence
on the verge—
the years having left
my wretched body
in the lurch.
Where there's one thing,
I now see four,
and whatever I hear
is thicker than stone.
Children jeer at me,
as do young ladies
comely and kind.
All this owing
to my piecemeal
loss of mind.
God grant us all
a merciful end.

HARDSHIPS I NOW ENDURE

1.

From Barbary to Araby
from Armenia to Persia
from Tartary to Syria
from Byzantium to Turkey
and on into Georgia—
I can no longer make these leaps.
Through Prussia, Russia, Estonia,

Lithuania, Livonia, along the strand
to Denmark, Sweden, and Brabant
through Flanders, France, England
and on into Scotland I went
without rest, league after league.
Through Aragon and Castile,
Granada and Navarra,
from Portugal and Galicia,
to Cabo Finisterre,
Provence and Marseilles.
And here in Ratzes-by-Schlern
I now sit against my will
watching my sorrow, ill
with my married state.
On this tiny outcrop of rock,
besieged by forests,
mountains high and valleys deep,
with each day nothing new to see
save stones, shrubs, snowstakes, stumps.
But what really gets on my nerves
is the racket my brats here make,
driving and drilling into my ears
(the last thing I deserve).

2.
All the honors bestowed on me
by sundry princes and queens,
all the good times I have seen,
I now atone for here beneath this roof.
My misery knows no end.
I need to get my wits about me,
since I have to scrounge for bread

and parry threats from every side,
with no red lips to console me.
With those who once obeyed me
I'm forced to contend.
Wherever I look, I'm aghast
at the scum all this former
loveliness has now become.
Where once were friends,
I now see calves,
goats, rams, steers, yokels
dumb as clogs,
black and coarse,
and, come winter,
full of snot—
not even to cows
would you dish out
this sort of slop.
I feel so cornered I get ornery
and start slapping around my tots.
Then their mother comes storming in
and proceeds to cuss me out
(if she chose to go at me
with fists, for sure I'd feel her clout).
She screams, "How dare you
pound our brats into flatcake."
I tremble at her rage,
unable to escape its range,
so sharp it splitteth me in twain.

3.
My pastimes here are most diverse.
Donkey-songs and peacock-screams:
what more could one ask of the universe?

The *hurlahei* of the stream
so rushes through my head
that it cleaves my skull in two.
These are the hardships I endure.
Hauenstein my home
isn't free from the bruise
of daily cares and rotten news.
Could I simply effect a change,
could someone come
bail me out,
I'd forever be in his debt.
My lord the Duke hounds me
because I've earned the envy
of all the local dreck.
My services are no longer welcome
(which gets under my skin),
this despite the fact
that no other dynasty
(here I give my word of honor)
ever did me any harm,
be it to body, name, or property
in the splendor of their domain.
My friends all hate me for no good cause,
which has hastened my old age.
To the world at large I complain—
to those most decent and wise,
to all those noble lords
who never used to mind
all my praises, all my hymns.
May they keep poor Wolkenstein
from being torn apart by wolves
and scattered to the winds.

ATTEMPTS UPON MY LIFE

1.

Whatever I sing or make into verse
about the dire consequences
of life on earth
strikes me as null and void

when I turn my thoughts to Death,
whom, traveling through the world,
I never managed to avoid.
He has often tried to take my life;
I've often escaped him by a hair.
Without throwing down the gauntlet,
he drives us to despair
with his cruel tricks—so quick
to catch us in his snares—
and has no room for patience
as he falls upon his prey.
Had I not outrun him,
he'd have already
snatched me away.
Be it on land or on sea,
on horseback or on foot,
he has laid his traps for me
and caught me in his snares.
Had I a sultan's treasure,
I'd offer it to him for free,
if, at my own pace,
he'd just let me be.
Counting all my falls,
all my near drownings,
and all my large deep wounds,
I've had seven attempts upon my life
and still hold no guarantee
I'll ever get off scot-free.
Death takes his meals beside me.
God knows how he finds me.

2.
I'll tell the true story
of the first of my calamities.
During a tournament,
on horseback,
I aimed my lance
and missed my man
and in my pique
plunged through a door
three feet wide
and a fathom deep
and crashed down
some twenty-four steps
to the cellar floor
where my poor horse
broke his neck.
I ended up
in a barrel of wine
and was fast sinking
so I invited my friends in
to help with the drinking.
A few weeks later,
God showed his favor.
In a storm my ship
got smashed to bits
but I managed
to lash onto
a cask of fine
Malvasia wine
and floated safely
ashore.

After my time at sea
this was the gift
that awaited me
when I got home.
To be promptly thrown
into a dungeon
and stripped
of all I owned.
My ears rang
with all the blows
rained down on me.
And someone half
skewered me
with a sword.

3.
Then there was the time
I tried to learn to swim
in a deep lake,
but once in,
shot straight
to the floor,
out of sight
for an hour or more.
Nice and cold down there,
looking for fish
with my nose tip.
But then I fell for her,
hook, line, and sinker,
and that little stinker
netted me

like a common thief,
she whom I held so dear
to heart, leaving me
awriggle in the ache
and grief of Love.
Far better
had she died
before my swim.
All she does
is do me in.
I learned this
as I rode to Hungary
in service of my Lady.
Still alone,
still accident-prone
on the flooded roads
(learning some Magyar—ha!—
along the way),
I nearly met my end
at the *tavakkal*
waterfall
that plunges down
from lofty cliffs.
A fool, I pitched
over its lip
and fell into the pool
where I splashed around
and nearly drowned,
wet to the bone.
I'd bet any precious stone,
however well-buffed,

however well-cut,
that no man in a hundred
could survive such
reckless plunges
into Love.

4.
Two and a half years later,
things took a turn for the worse.
I wanted to travel to foreign lands
to Portugal and the Barbary coast,
Granada and the Spanish main,
where I had high hopes
of being wildly entertained.
But my luck ran out.
A highborn Duke
named Friedrich,
displeased with me,
clapped me into jail,
innocent of any crime.
I thought my days on earth
had come and gone.
But since God
upon his throne most high
lets nothing go unpunished,
there I stayed
and paid my dues
and did my time.
My thanks also extend
to my old flame
for all the tunes

to which I set
my aches and pains,
though it was some years ago
that Death swept her away.
Let the hail trample
my memories of her,
let angry bears claw away
her every trace,
a potion too bitter
to the taste.
Had I only
overcooked my Love
on red-hot coals
and burnt it all away,
my tripes would be
less upset today.
These, at least, would be safe—
my life, my soul, my honor
and the extent of my estates.

5.
There's more I could say
but I'll spare you the tales
of all my adventures
with Christers, Russians, Greeks,
and heathens in my youth.
Now ridden by age,
these things no longer amuse.
How well-prepared will I be
when He of whom I spoke
cuts short my days

and snatches me away?
When the Judge comes
at me with his whip,
how filled with dread will I be?
What will be my fate?
Therefore, noble lords and squires,
take heed, you need
no advice from me.
You see how things proceed.
All of you, rich and poor alike,
should purify yourselves of sin,
lest Death come creeping in
and fall upon you on a whim.
O World, I always wonder
why you agree to be deceived,
you who see, day after day,
how Death puts us all to flight
from all our earthly delights.
Today you take your pick,
and tomorrow you'll die,
your name and fame all in vain,
until you face the music.

FAT TUESDAY

1.
Fat Tuesday shall soon be here,
time to feast, time to love,
couples wandering off
in good cheer,
cooing and billing
like turtledoves.

Me, I've got a hot date
with the crutch
my beloved gave me
as a mate, it's so sweet,
so tender to the touch.

> *When I take this crutch*
> *into the crotch*
> *of my arm*
> *and drive it home,*
> *she goes wild*
> *at my touch—*
> *can't help but groan.*
> *What better way*
> *to spend Mardi Gras*
> *alone. Basta!*
> *Enough with the moans!*

2.
Now that the birds
of the wild
have paired off
two by two,
why shouldn't
all these mild
young folk
kick off their shoes
and grab a girl
to kiss and pet?
Sweetheart,
give us a bite.

Steal some good times
from your tender
flesh. Girl,
you know it's all right.

> *When I take this crutch*
> *into the crotch*
> *of my arm*
> *and drive it home,*
> *she goes wild*
> *at my touch—*
> *can't help but groan.*
> *What better way*
> *to spend Mardi Gras*
> *alone. Basta!*
> *Enough with the moans!*

3.
Mardi Gras
and May so green
pipe forth
the same old tune.
What was buried
during the year
bursts by eyefuls
into bloom.
But my lady
managed to hide
her cruel designs
behind her smiles
until last fall.

Her treachery
I here decry,
now that I
must go lame.

When I take this crutch
into the crotch
of my arm
and drive it home,
she goes wild
at my touch—
can't help but groan.
What better way
to spend Mardi Gras
alone. Basta!
Enough with the moans!

BRING ON THE MORELS
AND CHANTERELLES

1.
Come on now, one
and all together,
man and wife and kids,
birds of a feather,
dance and leap,
harp and sing

to welcome in
the sweet green
gardens of spring.
The calls of thrush
and nightingale
echo through
hill and dale.
To pair off as two,
sneak a kiss,
and bill and coo—
far more fun
than soaking up
the sun

> *Let's shun*
> *the come-*
> *hither looks*
> *of ladies*
> *ungenteel,*
> *sweet nothings*
> *from pert little mouths*
> *make the finest meal.*

2.
Upward, little shrub,
outward, little herb,
Oesli and Gredli
into the tub!
Flower blossoms
O'erbower our bottoms,
rub-a-dub-dub.

Come, Metzli,
prepare our bath!
On with the fun:
"Wash my head,
my little love."
"Soap my tummy,
my little dove!
Help me with my little hole,
I'll help your little mole."

> *Let's shun*
> *the come-*
> *hither looks*
> *of ladies*
> *ungenteel,*
> *sweet nothings*
> *from pert little mouths*
> *make the finest meal.*

3.
Hooray, hooray!
O lovely May!
Bring on the morels
and chanterelles.
To man, grass, and tree,
to hind, hare, and beast
bring on the delights
of all this green,
of all that winter
drove away
and buried deep

behind the walls
and deadened with deceit,
O May, release it all,
responding to our call.

> *Let us shun*
> *the come-*
> *hither looks*
> *of ladies*
> *ungenteel,*
> *sweet nothings*
> *from pert little mouths*
> *make the finest meal.*

THY KNIGHT IN JAIL

Bog dep'mi / was dustu da   [Slovenian/German]
gramer sici ty / sine cura   [Provençal/Latin]
Ich fraw mich zwar / q'video te   [German/Latin]
cu[m] bonavnor / jassem toge   [Provençal/Slovenian]
Dut mi sperancz / nate str[v?]oio   [Provençal/Slovenian]
wan[n] dus bist glancz / cu[m] gaudeo [German/Latin]
Op[er]a m[e]a / ich dir halt   [Latin/German]
nodobrisi slusba / bass calt.   [Provençal/Slovenian]

> Welcome! What brings thee here?
> Free from care, I thank thee dear.
> Delighted to lay eyes on thee again,
> To feel love as way back when.
> All my hope goes out to thee,
> Light of my life, with joy redeemed.
> I'll stand by thee with every deed,
> Serving thee in thy every need.

Ka cu mores / mich mach[en] mat   [French/German]
chage sum press / hoc me mirat   [Provençal/Latin]
Bedenk dein gnad / c[um] pietas   [German/Latin]
negam maluat / nemon dilass   [Provençal/French]
kiti cu[m] mand / en iassem dyal   [Provençal/Slovenian]
wo ichs bekant / abo[mni] mal   [German/Latin]
Hoc des me / geniss[en] lan   [Latin/German]
troge moye / cu[m] bon wan[n] an.   [Slovenian/Provençal]

> *How thou makest me weak and pale*
> *Amazeth me, thy knight in jail.*
> *Try taking some mercy on me,*
> *Keep me from the path of adversity.*
> *Thy wish shall be my command*
> *If it entails nothing wrong.*
> *Good wishes, lady, let me hear*
> *This bright day of a bright new year.*

Jo te prosso / dein genad all da   [Italian/German]
gesi grando / er opti[m]a   [Provençal/Latin]
Halt mich nit sw[er] / h[o]c rogo te   [German/Latin]
qo p[r]ope[n]sar / nate troge   [Provençal/Italian]
Flore wellenpiank / pomag menne   [Italian/Slovenian]
das ich dir dank / cu[m] fidele   [German/Latin]
no[n] fac' hoc / so bin ich tod   [Latin/German]
sellennem tlok / sit tutel rot.   [Slovenian/Italian]

> *Grant me thy grace, without falsity,*
> *Show me largesse, out of courtesy.*
> *Don't make things hard, think of me*
> *As I consider thee, with amity.*

A spray of white flowers, against misery,
A gift to thee, for thy loyalty.
Do this soon, or I'll be dead,
And quit these green woods in greatest dread.

DO IT IN TONGUES!

1.

Do fraig amors,	[French]	*Dearest love,*
adiuva me!	[Latin]	*assist me!*
Malout, mein pferd	[Hungarian, German]	*My horse, my steed*
Nai moi sercce,	[Slovenian]	*wherewith my heart*
rennt mit gedanck,	[German]	*runs, thanks*
frau, pur äti.	[German, Italian]	*lady, to thee.*
Eck lopp, eck slapp,	[Flemish]	*I walk, I sleep,*
vel quo vado	[Latin]	*wherever I go*
wesegg mein krap	[Hungarian]	*my anchor is*
ne dirs dobro.	[Slovenian]	*barely aweigh.*
Ju gslaff	[Slovenian]	*Free to stray*
ee franck	[Italian]	*into the me-*
merschi vois gri.	[French]	*mory of thee.*

Refrain:
Do it in German! And Italian!
Wake up in French!
In Hungarian, laugh!
Bake bread in Slovenian!
In Flemish, call!
Add Latin: seven tongues in all!

2.

Mille schenna,	[Slovenian]	*Sweet lady,*
ime,	[Hungarian]	*see here*
man gür,	[French]	*my heart,*
Peromnia	[Latin]	*throughout*
meins leibes spür.	[German]	*my body's trace.*
Cenza befiw	[Italian]	*In every place*
met gschoner war	[Flemish]	*of thy beauty*
dut servirai,	[Italian]	*I serve thy*
pur tschätti gaiss	[Slovenian]	*pure desire*
nem tudem	[Hungarian]	*in everything,*
frai	[French]	*free*
kain falsche rais.	[German]	*from dishonesty.*
Got wett wol, twiv	[Flemish]	*God knows*
eck de amar.	[Latin]	*I do love thee.*

Refrain:
Do it in German! And Italian!
Wake up in French!
In Hungarian, laugh!
Bake bread in Slovenian!
In Flemish, call!
Add Latin: seven tongues in all!

3.

De mit mundesch	[Hungarian]	*Whatever thou wishest,*
Margarita bell,	[Italian]	*my lovely Gret,*
Exprofundis	[Latin]	*ex profundis,*
das tün ich snell.	[German]	*I'm on it now.*
dat löff,	[Flemish]	*Believe me,*
draga Griet,	[Slovenian]	*dear Gretl,*
Permafo!	[French]	*cross my heart!*
In recommisso	[Latin]	*Under thy spell,*
diors ee nöt	[French]	*day and night,*
mi ti commando,	[Italian]	*I wish thee well,*
wo ich trtot.	[German]	*wherever I go,*
jambre,	[Hungarian]	*my love,*
twoia,	[Slovenian]	*and thine,*
allopp mi troi.	[Flemish]	*forever twined.*

Refrain:
Do it in German! And Italian!
Wake up in French!
In Hungarian, laugh!
Bake bread in Slovenian!
In Flemish, call!
Add Latin: seven tongues in all!

Notes to the poems

WAR MUSIC *("Nu Huss! sprach der Michel von Wolkenstein," K. 85)*. Composed in 1423. Although written somewhat later than the poems that follow, I have placed this song first, in homage to Ezra Pound's celebrated "Sestina: Alta-forte," a translation of Bertran de Born's song in praise of war. Like Bertran, whom Dante placed in Malebolge among "the stirrers up of strife," O. was a notable sower of discord. In this poem he records the siege of the castle of Greifenstein, where he, his brothers, and other local lords were holed up in open feudal rebellion against the administrative centralization of the region under Frederick IV, Duke of Austria and Count of Tyrol.

KNIGHT ERRANT *("Es fuegt sich," K. 18)*. O.'s most famous retrospect on his life, written when he was more or less forty. This song was most likely composed and performed in Constance in 1417 for the amusement of the large group of German-speaking political dignitaries and influential clerics assembled there for the Church Council organized by King Sigismund. The poem is divided into seven sixteen-line stanzas, rhymed AAAbCCCbDDDDbEEEb, with multiple ingenious *Binnenreime* (or internal rhymes). A superb recording of this song by the countertenor Andreas Scholl is available on YouTube.

2 *Ruprecht*: King Rupert, King of the Germans and *Rex Romanorum* (reign: 1400–1410).
Sigmund: Rupert's successor Sigismund (reign: 1411–1437).
Moorish: I.e. Arabic, which O. may have acquired during his pilgrimage to the Holy Land or while participating in the 1415 Portuguese conquest of the Moorish stronghold of Ceuta in North Africa.
Wendish: Language spoken in neighboring Slovenia, as well as on the southern coast of the Baltic and in areas west of the Elbe River (where it is sometimes called Sorbian).
Lombard: The language spoken in northern Italy, directly south of the Tyrol.
Romansch: Or Ladino, late Latin dialect spoken in the adjacent Swiss canton of Graubünden, as well as in certain valleys of the Dolomites.

3 *non maiplus disligaides*: "Never remove it" (in the Iberian dialect spoken at the courts of Aragon).

Pedro Luna: I.e., antipope Benedict XIII, whom Sigismund visited in Perpignan in 1415 in order to strong-arm him into renouncing his claims to the papacy and thus bring an end to the Western Schism.

the tenth Roman king: Sigismund.

the lady of Prades: Margaret of Prades (1395–1429), widowed Queen Consort of Aragon.

4 *A Lady (whom I'd rather not name)*: Anna Hausmann. Named only once in O.'s poetry as "die Hausmannin."

6 *Ios land*: Island in the Greek Cyclades, probably visited by O. during his pilgrimage to the Holy Land in 1409–10.

7 *My wife*: Margarete von Schwangau (1390 –c. 1451), whom O. officially wed in her castle in Bavaria in the summer of 1417.

PENANCE *("Ain anefangt," K. 1)*. Written between 1421 and 1422. The first of seven prison poems (K. 1–K. 7) that O. placed at the incipit of both Ms. A (1425) and Ms. B (1432), all of which are composed in the same strophic mode and to the same tune. This inaugural K. 1 complaint seems to telescope O.'s first imprisonment by Jäger in Meran (October–December 1421) and his second imprisonment by Frederick in Innsbruck (December 1421–March 1422).

2 *thirteen years or more*: This would seem to indicate that it was in 1407 or 1408—the year he dedicated a chapel to his patron saint Oswald at the Brixen monastery—that O. first met Anna Hausmann, the duplicitous Dark Lady who subsequently laid the trap that allowed Jäger (with whom some scholars suggest she may have also been romantically involved) to clap him into prison in Meran thirteen years later.

MERCIFUL END *("Ich sich und hör," K. 5)*. The same melodic and strophic arrangement as the previous song, which affiliates it with the melancholic, melismatic music of his prison poems of 1421–22, although its composition may date as late as his residence in Neuhaus in 1425. O. is a mere forty-eight when he has this *Alterslied* (or traditional "old-age song") transcribed by the Neustift monks in Ms. A.

HARDSHIPS I NOW ENDURE *("Durch, Barbarei, Arabia," K. 44)*. Probably composed in the winter of 1426–27 at Hauenstein, shortly before O.'s final arrest by Frederick and imprisonment at Vellenberg in Innsbruck. Another attempt to retrospectively construct a first-person epic of his Odyssean life, beginning with the early adventures of his youth, his pilgrimage to the Holy Land, his diplomatic travels with King Sigismund, and his final *nostos* to Hauenstein, "this tiny outcrop of rock," near the village of Ratzes, just east of the Schlern massif.

ATTEMPTS UPON MY LIFE *("Wie vil ich sing und tichte," K. 23)*. Most likely composed in 1427.

2 *Malvasia*: Group of grape varieties grown historically in the Mediterranean region, the Balearic Islands, and the island of Madeira, but not to be confused with sweet Malmsey, or Madeira wine. Among the wares that, according to poem II ("Knight Errant"), O. was transporting by boat during his early travels as a merchant in the eastern Mediterranean and the Black Sea. Cf. Stefano in *The Tempest*, II, 2: "I escaped upon a butt of sack which the sailors heaved o'erboard, by this bottle, which I made of the bark of a tree, with mine own hands since I was cast ashore."

3 *as I rode to Hungary / in service of my Lady*: O. first traveled to Hungary / Bohemia in 1419 to join up with Sigismund.
tavakkal: Hungarian for lake, marsh, pond.

4 *two and a half years later*: Probably refers to his imprisonment by Frederick in Innsbruck in 1421–22.
though it was some years ago / that Death swept her away: Anna Hausmann, the Dark Lady, died in 1425.

FAT TUESDAY *("Es nahent gein der vasennacht," K. 60)*. A rollicking goliardic *Fastnacht*, or Mardi Gras, song, which scholars date to O.'s imprisonment in the spring of 1422, given that it alludes, in its third section, to Anna Hausmann's role in luring him into Jäger's prison ambush that previous fall.

BRING ON THE MORELS AND CHANTERELLES *("Wol auf, wol an,"* K. 75)*. A typical *Mailied*, or May Day Song, probably written in 1422, after his release from prison and now clearly delighted to rediscover the vernal delights of his wife, "Gredli." In section two, for reasons of rhyme, I have translated "rat" (which is how O. usually refers to his penis) as "mole."

THY KNIGHT IN JAIL *("Bog dep'mi was dustu da," K.119)*. The standard topos of the unrequited lover as the metaphorical slave (or prisoner) of his Dark Lady. Probably written in Constance in 1417, that is, before O. had actually spent any time in jail. A poem notable for its polyglot blend of troubadour Provençal, Latin, French, Italian, German, and Slovenian (i.e. Wendish).

DO IT IN TONGUES! *("Do frayg amors / adiuva me," K. 69)*. A New Year's Song, also probably composed at the Council of Constance in 1417 for a multilingual German audience who would have appreciated O.'s macaronic mash-up of seven tongues (German, Italian, French, Hungarian, Slovenian, Flemish, and Latin) in a poem for which he also provides an *exposicio* ("exposition" or "translation") into Middle High German.